When You Are Suffering

Books in This Series:

When Things Go Wrong
When You Are Afraid
When You Are Suffering
When You Have Doubts

When You Are Suffering

A Book of Comfort

Alvin N. Rogness

Augsburg

MINNEAPOLIS

WHEN YOU ARE SUFFERING
A Book of Comfort
by Alvin N. Rogness

1999 Augsburg Books Edition.

Text of this edition originally appeared in *Book of Comfort,* Copyright © 1979 Augsburg Publishing House.

Cover design by Craig Claeys; interior design by Michelle L. Norstad.

Acknowledgments
Scripture quotations are from the New Revised Standard Version © 1989 by the Division of Christian Education of the National Council of the Churches of Christ in the United States of America. Used by permission.

Library of Congress Cataloging-in-Publication Data

Rogness, Alvin N., 1906-
    When you are suffering : a book of comfort / by Alvin N. Rogness. —
Augsburg Books ed.
    p. cm.
    Includes bibliographical references.
    ISBN 0-8066-3839-7 (alk. paper)
    1. Suffering—Religious aspects—Christianity. 2. Christian life—
Lutheran authors. 3. Consolation. I. Title.
BV4909.R65 1999
248.8'6—dc21   98-48281
                                               CIP

Manufactured in the U.S.A.   AF 9-3839

03   02   01   00   99   1   2   3   4   5   6   7   8   9   10

Contents

Preface
7

When Suffering Seems Meaningless
9

When Memories Haunt You
16

When You Can't Forgive
21

When You're Sick
26

When Prayers Go Unanswered
31

When Grief Won't Let Go
36

When Death Is at the Door
42

Preface

You and I are on a road of sharp turns and sudden dips. And there's fog, thick fog. Sometimes boulders block the way. We neglect the map and are lured into detours. Weary, we may want to give up. We cry for comfort.

There is comfort. Years ago God said,

> Comfort, comfort my people. . . .
> Speak tenderly to Jerusalem, and proclaim to her
> that her hard service has been completed,
> that her sin has been paid for,
> that she has received from the Lord's hand
> double for all her sins.

God yearns to comfort us—but on God's terms and in God's way. If I call on God, I understand that he may have to stop me in my tracks and turn me around before he can be gentle. God may have to use the scalpel before he can heal my pain.

In these short chapters I've tried to describe stretches along the road. I've traveled many of them. I'm old enough to have learned a little about them. But I'm no heroic traveler. Many times I've rejected God's comfort and tried to go it alone. Often I've been puzzled about the kind of comfort God seemed to give.

I have the map, the Word of God, God's wisdom and promises. And I have a Friend who has walked the way before me and who walks with me now. His hand is on me to lead me and to hold me. There is no greater comfort than that.

1

When Suffering
Seems Meaningless

Life is a jigsaw puzzle, a jumble of pieces that, try as we will, we'll never quite assemble into a clear picture. Most difficult to fit are the dark fragments of pain and evil and suffering. We wonder, Why are they needed at all? Has some impish elf smuggled them in to sabotage all attempts to make life meaningful?

We can understand suffering that comes directly from our wrongs or neglects. If I rob a bank and go to prison, if I betray a trust and lose my job, if I get drunk and drive off the road and languish in a hospital—these I can understand. But pain and tragedy sometimes have no clear connection with anything a person does or fails to do.

Why should my brother and his wife lose their Jimmy at fourteen and their Dianne at seventeen from brain tumors? Why should it have been our son who at twenty-four was struck down in a street accident? Why should my friend's lovely daughter become emotionally unbalanced and take her life just before her baby was to be born, and my cousin's brilliant son, in his first year at the university, lose his bearings and commit suicide? Why does a tornado destroy one farm and not another? Why should a hundred villages be devastated by a tidal wave?

Suffering strikes with reckless caprice. Many of the pieces simply do not fit. Job couldn't make them fit— remember? In what is perhaps the profoundest treatment of evil or suffering in all the world's literature, the Old Testament tells of this upright man who, in a swift succession of catastrophes, loses his property, his children, and his health. At first he's able to say "The Lord gave, and the Lord has taken away; blessed be the name of the Lord."

But as his pain continues, he begins to despair.

> Why was I not hidden in the ground like a stillborn
> child, like an infant who never saw the light of day?
> . . . I have been allotted months of futility, and nights
> of misery have been assigned to me. . . . The night
> drags on, and I toss till dawn.

Then he begins to address God,

Your hands shaped me and made me. Will you now
turn and destroy me? . . . Why then did you bring me
out of the womb? I wish I had died before any eye
saw me.

The amazing thing about Job is that, while challeng-
ing God to give him some answer, he retains a rugged
integrity.

As long as I have life within me . . . my lips will not
speak wickedness, and my tongue will utter no deceit
. . . till I die, I will not deny my integrity. I will main-
tain my righteousness and never let go of it; my conscience will not reproach me as long as I live.

This remarkable drama ends with Job still asking for an
answer, but with his trust in God unshaken.

One might try being indifferent to pain. But if you
deny pain in yourself, you must deny it in others, and the
springs of compassion dry up. Most of us will not settle
for that. We insist on trying to fit the pieces somewhere, to
find some meaning. Or, failing to fit them anywhere, we

will at least want to rescue some significance, or if not significance, some value.

The Book of Job does give one very important clue. God allows suffering, but he does not design it. God did not arrange to have our son killed. God did allow it. Why he allowed it, perhaps I will learn when I get to heaven, but surely not before. But it helps me to know that God did not engineer the accident.

Since God keeps me in the dark about the riddle of evil and suffering, the best I can do is to struggle with what I might do about it. Do I shake my fists at God, do I throw up my hands, do I collapse in sheer weariness? Or do I dig around in the debris and try to find something that can be rescued?

I'd rather explore what can be salvaged. I can think of at least three ways to find meaning in suffering.

The first is the way my brother dealt with the death of his two children. He pointed to the obvious gain. God gave him and Ruth the joy of their children for a total of thirty-one years. Would they in their deepest grief ever wish that they had never had them, so they could be spared their present pain? No. Moreover, he asked, isn't death but an incident, a small punctuation mark, in the larger dimensions of a life that is eternal? Despite their great grief, they had been able to find a place for the dark pieces of the puzzle.

Second, suffering may have a good effect on the person who suffers. The Jewish people have known great suffering and it is not uncommon for Jewish parents to acquaint their children early with the long history of the sufferings of their people—to prepare them for a similar fate, and, even more, to make them sensitive to the suffering of others. A tradition among the rabbinic schools of the Jewish people holds that only those who have known suffering themselves can understand and help those who suffer. We are not fully human until we have known suffering.

I am unable to tell whether the death of our Paul has made us more understanding of those who suffer. I think so. The bitterness I first felt I believe is gone, and I think we're better able "to weep with those who weep." If so, then the death of our son has had meaning.

The third way to make suffering meaningful is more mysterious. Pope John XXIII, when struck with cancer, offered his sufferings "for the peace of the world." He regarded his pain as a gift he had to give all humanity. I am intrigued by this idea. Can those who suffer make of the very sufferings something good? If those who suffer do not

13

protest and rebel, but accept pain as part of the human situation, can they give their gift to all people as an offering for the betterment of the world?

As members of the human family, we are not to be spared pain. We are not aristocrats, with an inalienable right to be happy. What the rest of the family suffers, you and I ought to suffer, to be part of them.

I am struck by these lines in Hebrews 12: "[Consider Jesus,] who for the joy that was set before him endured the cross, scorning its shame, and sat down at the right hand of the throne of God. . . . You have not yet resisted [suffered] to the point of shedding your blood."

If you feel sorry for yourself, says this writer in Hebrews, take a look at Jesus. He deserved no suffering, yet he suffered. You're no better than he. Somehow his suffering has ennobled the whole world. You and I suffering with him, with his absence of bitterness, may in some way also help to ennoble the world. We cannot approach his matchless patience, but we are invited to try.

We in America have been spared the colossal sufferings of other nations in this volcanic century. None of our cities are in rubble, our borders have not been invaded, we are not homeless refugees. Why have we been spared? That too is a part of the puzzle. Certainly not because we are such virtuous, self-denying people. Who among us dares to claim special rights before God?

If our lives have fallen on pleasant times, and if we have been spared tragedies that have fallen on others, are we not the more under obligation to serve those who have dark pieces in their lives?

The puzzle is still here. Why suffering, why pain, why evil, why death? Instead of being paralyzed by the puzzle, instead of giving up and throwing the dark pieces away, we are invited to lift our eyes to God.

We will have to wait for the final answers, but meanwhile God will help us find some place for the pieces.

And the God of all grace, who called you to his eternal glory in Christ, after you have suffered a little while, will himself restore you and make you strong, firm, and steadfast.
1 Peter 5:9–10

2

When Memories Haunt You

My life is full of memories. The good ones make up a company of cherished people and events of the past that, added to the present, give my life fullness.

The bad ones add a touch of sadness and melancholy. But they don't haunt me or crush me. I have learned how to deal with them. I could never have done it without God.

There are three kinds of bad memories. First, memories of unpleasant or even tragic events over which I had no control. Second, memories of wrongs done to me by others. And third, memories of wrongs I have done to others, or of the good I have failed to do for them.

The first kind of memory is not destructive, because such memories carry no guilt. A tornado or a fire destroys your home. The fluctuation of the stock market wipes out your assets. Diabetes claims your leg. An accident kills your friend. These traumatic events leave you struggling to get your bearings, but they are simply part of the human situation. You did not cause them. You need feel no remorse.

Memories of wrongs done to you by others may be more troublesome. Someone you loved rejected you. Your partner in business maneuvered you out of your holdings. Someone you had trusted sued you unjustly. You may have trouble erasing the memory and ridding yourself of bitterness, but the wrong was someone else's, not yours.

The memories of your own wrongs are the destructive ones. Try as you will to marshal extenuating circumstances to excuse yourself, you won't succeed. Try to push the memories under the rug, and they creep out to haunt you at the most unexpected moments. They demand that you deal with them.

If the people you have wronged are alive and within reach, you may make a direct approach. You may ask forgiveness and make what amends you can. If they are willing to accept your remorse and your efforts to mend the wrong, there will be healing. But often there's a roadblock. They cannot accept your pleas, or won't. The damage may be beyond repair. A man who has abandoned his family may never, try as he will, heal the wounds he has caused. A drunken driver cannot restore the life she crushed on the road. Every one of us has left a trail of wrongs, big and small, both by what we have done and by what we have failed to do. We will never be able to clear the road of all the debris. If we are sensitive at all, we carry a cargo of memories that threatens to crush us.

Unless—unless there is a place where we can dump the whole wretched load. And there is. That's where God comes in. Resting the load with God is not a "cop-out." It's rather as if a person has all sorts of bills hanging over him, and he goes to the bank and gets one loan and his new debtor (the bank) enables him to come to terms with all the others. This may be an inadequate parallel, but the Lord's sweeping forgiveness is just this kind of miracle.

There will be dangling ends, hurts that will never be healed until we die. But at the center of life, at the heart of the universe, in God who gave us life—the whole sorry stuff is removed as far as the east is from the west. We have the staggering assurance, "Your sins will I remember no more." And the memories we carry will have lost their power to destroy us. Moreover, we will have not only the right, but the duty, to forget them too!

In his *Macbeth*, Shakespeare has Lord and Lady Macbeth murder Duncan, the king. In the aftermath, Lady Macbeth's conscience drives her mad. Lord Macbeth comes to the doctor with the plea,

> Canst thou not minister to a mind diseased,
> Pluck from the memory a rooted sorrow,
> Raze out the written troubles of the brain,
> And with some sweet oblivious antidote
> Cleanse the stuffed bosom of that perilous stuff
> That weighs upon the heart?

The doctor says, "More needs she the divine than the physician. God, God forgive us all!"

All the frantic distractions we contrive, all the skills of the psychologist, all the sedation of alcohol and drugs cannot remove the memories of our wrongs. There is no sweet oblivious antidote to cleanse the stuffed bosom of the perilous stuff of guilt—except the miracle of God's forgiveness in Christ and the cross.

The profound secret of this healing is the fact that all wrongs against other people are finally wrongs against the God who gave us life and who redeems us. King David committed adultery with Uriah's wife Bathsheba and engi-

19

neered Uriah's death. When brought to repentance, David cried to God, "Against you, you only, have I sinned and done what is evil in your sight." He could not bring Uriah back to life; he would make no amends by abandoning Bathsheba. There was but one place where he could find healing—in the mercy of God.

You don't play the coward and pass the buck when you bring your wretched memories and guilt to the foot of the cross. The Lord himself invites you to leave them there. You will still have scars, but the festering wounds will be gone. You stand before God as if you had never sinned. Finally, you are free to bask in all the good memories you have. And you have many!

> *Forgetting what is behind and straining toward what is ahead,*
> *I press on toward the goal to win the prize for which God has*
> *called me heavenward in Christ Jesus.*
> *Philippians 3:13–14*

3

When You Can't Forgive

I sat with two of my friends. One had grievously wronged the other.

When John said, "I will never forgive you" I told him, "I won't let you say *will never*. I'll let you say *can never*, because on your own I don't think you can. But there is a power that can help you. That's what this whole business of Christianity is about."

I don't know whether he ever forgave, but he understood. He knew that if he were to take Christ seriously, he couldn't decide never to forgive. He had to be open to the miracle.

If I were Jewish and my parents and brothers and sisters had been executed in Hitler's ovens, could I ever forgive? Could I join Jesus in saying, "Father, forgive them, for they do not know what they are doing"? Maybe, but if so, it would be a sheer miracle of spirit. More than likely, until I died I'd have to ask Christ to forgive me for not being able to forgive.

Most of us will never have to deal with Hitler. But life will be full of wrongs that hurt, some little, some big. Whether thoughtlessly or deliberately, people will wrong us, and we will wrong them. And every wrong is a link in a chain of bitterness and hatred that binds us and robs us of joy. It's a poison that eats away at our hearts.

There are wrongs so trivial that they need not distress you. Someone seems to snub you. Someone forgot to thank you. They left your name out of the paper. They forgot your birthday. They never sent you a card when you were in the hospital. If you let these little things bother you, you're on the way to what the psychologists call paranoia. You enjoy self-pity. In almost all such instances the oversights were unintentional. Forgive them and forget them.

But there are real wrongs. Your husband becomes enamored of another woman and has an affair. Your wife becomes an alcoholic and your home life is soon in shambles. Your partner in business maneuvers you out of the company. You thought someone was your friend, but you

22

learn that he has misrepresented facts about you to squeeze you out of a job. A relative who could have helped you out of a jam simply let you down.

Evil is afoot in the world, in our hearts and in the hearts of all. There is none really good, through and through. Try as we will, we will struggle with the Mr. Hyde, the dark forces of our natures. Our goals and our motives will be a bewildering mix of the good and bad, the unselfish and selfish. We will wrong others by what we do and by what we fail to do, no matter how vigilant we are.

You dare not set out to forgive someone unless you understand that you too need forgiveness. If you can't admit that you need to be forgiven, any forgiveness you may presume to give will be nothing more than condescension, patronage, at best, pity. From your high and mighty station of purity, you look down—probably with disdain—on the person to be forgiven. This kind of forgiveness is more cruel than none at all.

It was John Bradford who, watching someone being led to the gallows, said, "There but for the grace of God go I." You may not be able to put yourself in the place of persons who have wronged you, but you will need to try—if you are to be able to forgive. What drove them to do these things? Were they more susceptible to such weaknesses than you are? What strengths may the Lord have given you through the years that they failed to develop? Having favored you with strength, does the Lord expect you to carry some of their weaknesses? You can't dismiss the wrong by saying, "They couldn't help it." Nonetheless, people do vary in the natures and heritages and faculties they have.

You might even ask, "Are they happy in what they have done to me?" Who, in the long run, suffers most? When the Scriptures point out that it is better to suffer wrong than to inflict wrong, they direct us to a profound secret of life. What uneasy conscience, what fleeting advantage, what questionable pleasure may come from doing wrong, com-pared with the profound joys that come from being able to forgive wrongs?

But you ask, "How can I forgive them if they do not want forgiveness?" All you can do is be ready and willing to forgive. Until people face their wrong and show some indi-cation that they want forgiveness and reconciliation, the road is blocked—for them, not for you. You may rid your heart of the poison of resentment, hatred, bitterness, and wait the moment when your gift of forgiveness can be delivered.

We'll never get far with forgiving one another unless we understand that we are embraced by our Lord in his love and forgiveness, as wide as the wideness of the sea. If we start there, as the forgiven of God, he can let us in on the joy of becoming the forgiving ones. We may then discover, as George Macdonald has said, that to forgive is the luxury of the Christian's life.

> *Be kind and compassionate to one another, forgiving each other,*
> *just as in Christ God forgave you.*
> *Ephesians 4:32*

4

When You're Sick

I had usually thanked God for health and prayed that he might keep me from being ill. One evening, while speaking in a church, I suddenly collapsed. For two weeks I rested in a hospital waiting for my duodenal ulcer to stop bleeding.

I don't remember thinking that if I had stronger faith the bleeding would stop, or that someone with the gift of healing could lay hands on my head and make it stop. I relied on the skills that the Lord had given his servants, the doctors, and on the recuperative powers God had placed in my body. Of course I prayed for healing. Who doesn't when ill? You may have forgotten to pray for almost anything, but you do look to God when illness strikes. Even people who have trouble taking God's intervention seriously at all will pray in a crisis. From World War One came the refrain,

"There are not atheists in foxholes." There is an old Russian proverb *Kak trevoga, tak do boga*—"In dire extremity man remembers his God."

I had no trouble thanking God for restoring my health, and I didn't bother my mind about whether it was through the science of medicine (which is God's) or through the healing power of my body (which is God's), or whether God intervened in some special way.

God is on the side of life and health. If I understand Scripture right, God intended us for everlasting life, uninterrupted by death. God did not want us to be sick and die. Sin and sickness and death are intruders. I've never hesitated to urge the sick to pray for health. I think we're on God's side when we do everything possible to guard the gift of life and health.

God's plan is that sin and illness and death will at last be destroyed. Until that moment comes, God allows death to be the gateway through which we pass to inherit a life that is unending. We have no guarantee that we will outmaneuver death and live forever on this side, no matter how many healers we employ. Even Jesus, who brought back from the dead Lazarus, the widow's son at Nain, and Jairus' daughter, did not give them eternal tenure on this side.

27

Eventually they did have to die.

Think of the comfort of healing God has given us in the last century through the spectacular advances in medical science. Many of the old killers—smallpox, diphtheria, peritonitis, pneumonia—are virtually gone.

Most doctors will say that they only remove or correct obstructions that keep the body from doing its own healing work. But often we don't cooperate with God in allowing the recuperative powers of our own bodies to take effect. We overeat. We drink damaging beverages. We fail to exercise.

When I became sick, I took stock of my neglects. I had plunged ahead in my work, been neglectful of rest and sleep, and in other ways ignored the rights of my body. How could I expect God to keep me well if I defied his laws?

How about God's direct intervention through extraordinary means? Are there "divine healers"? The New Testament seems to indicate that God does give the gift of healing to certain people. And many people are sure that the Lord has, through these people, intervened in ways beyond the reach of science or the normal recuperative powers of the body.

When one of my friends was ill with a puzzling dis-

ease, people urged his wife to summon some person with a
reputation for healing. She hesitated to summon anyone.
Hundreds, even thousands, of people were already pleading
with God for his healing. She asked herself, What kind of a
God would ignore the prayers of thousands and sit
unmoved in his heavens, withholding healing till some
"assigned" person came? She said, "I'd have to change my
whole idea of a merciful God if I were to think that he
would let my husband die unless a 'special' person prayed."

On the other hand, there is the testimony of many people who believe firmly that God has used some person
other than the doctor for special healing. Perhaps this is
one of the mysteries we'll have to live with.

As we desire healing and life, we must try to keep illness in the right perspective. We know that life on this side
is uncertain. We know too that the excellence of a life is
not measured by its length, any more than the excellence of
a painting depends on the size of the canvas. We live in the
anticipation of life everlasting on the other side, which a
gracious God in love and forgiveness has promised us in
Christ Jesus.

To be sick puts you on trial. To be on your back in the
hospital, in pain and perhaps with scant hope of recovery,

29

is the hardest assignment life has given you. If you are able to exercise patience, love, cheerfulness, a sense of humor, and hope in such an hour, you may have given your family and friends the most treasured memories they'll ever have. If God can help you do that, your measure of comfort will be sublime.

Heal me, O Lord, and I will be healed; save me and I will be saved.

Jeremiah 17:14

5

When Prayers Go Unanswered

If you were headed in the wrong direction, on a road where a bridge had been washed out by a raging torrent, you wouldn't expect God to help you get there. You could rather count on God putting every possible roadblock in the way so that, discouraged, you'd turn around.

We often make the mistake of calling on God to comfort us in what we are doing, when above all else he wants to disturb us. He would be less than a loving God if he didn't.

God's goal with each of us is to shape us up into the kind of people we ought to be as his children. God knows that nothing short of that will really fulfill the deepest longings and yearnings of our spirit. The Good Shepherd sends fierce sheep dogs to harass us until we turn back to the fold. It's futile to ask him to call off the dogs until we change direction.

God does want us to have what we need. He taught us to pray, "Give us this day our daily bread," which Luther says includes everything that is required to satisfy our temporal needs, such as food, clothing, shelter, families, good government, good weather, true friends, peace, and health. In an affluent nation such as ours we tend to expand these needs into security and pleasure far beyond any sensible standard.

One evening a recurrent advertisement punctuated our TV program, proposing that we buy a weekend excursion to Las Vegas. The punch line was, "You need it and you deserve it." Since our Minnesota windchill temperature at that moment was fifty degrees below zero, it wasn't difficult to agree that we needed a breather in warm weather, and we could even conclude that we deserved it as much as our neighbors who had just left for Hawaii. If the Lord was listening in, he must have chuckled (or wept) at the nonsense of redefining our needs to include Las Vegas. But our whole culture is victimized by such distortion.

Isn't it safe to conclude that the Lord wants no part in making us wealthy, unless we use this wealth in the service of others, or that he deplores our gaining office or power unless we use such influence for the welfare of all? God's only interest in our attaining wealth or power is what effect, for good or ill, it might have on us. If possessions tend to make us proud and self-indulgent, we could expect him to take them away.

Probably our whole way of life has to be measured by spiritual objectives. If it's harder for God to bring us around to his way with jets and computers, he might favor our going back to donkeys and the abacus.

It takes unusual grace to believe that when something goes wrong with our plans, it might be that God is administering his kind of comfort. Speaking of adversities, the writer in Hebrews tells us, "God is treating you as sons. For what son is not disciplined by his father? No discipline seems pleasant at the time, but painful. Later on, however, it produces a harvest of righteousness and peace for those who have been trained by it."

Most of us will not take this counsel as literally as the old missionary who, upon getting sick, was cheered that God had not forgotten him but was now spanking him a little. It would be folly to conclude that every time we run into adversity—sickness, loss of a job, collapse of invest-

ments, election defeat, rejection, the death of a loved one—
that God is spanking us. God suffers with us. But if we will
let him, God can use adversities to good ends for us. They
can prod us to reexamine what is important, and help us to
shift our priorities. God has done it again and again.

When we lost our son at twenty-four, we realized that
for twenty-five years our family had suffered no major
hurts. Suddenly we became aware of our many friends who
were also burdened with tragedies. It was as if we were no
longer set apart as "special," but had become part of the
human family in which misfortunes and sorrows are built
into life. Grief-stricken as we were, this thought brought
strange comfort. Our prayers for his safety had not been
answered, but something good was emerging for us.

The worst thing that can happen to us is that we can go
on blithely in our preoccupation with self, relatively
untouched by reversals, growing complacent, a bit proud,
and quite indifferent to the suffering world. God has little
chance to reach us, because we will not cry to him. We may
even forget to thank him.

34   If God doesn't specifically arrange our adversities, he
may indeed allow them to happen—for our own good, and
for our eventual comfort.

Consider it pure joy, my brothers, whenever you face trials of many kinds, because you know that the testing of your faith develops perseverance. Perseverance must finish its work so that you may be mature and complete, not lacking anything.

James 1:2–4

6

When Grief Won't Let Go

I knew grief when my father and mother died the same summer at sixty-six, but that grief lifted. It was different when our son was killed at twenty-four.

My parents' death left me sad to think that I had no one to write to about the joys of their grandchildren. I realized that now I was on the top rung of the ladder of the generations, and it was lonely up there. I no longer had the luxury of being someone's child.

Twelve years later our Paul's life was snuffed out on a city street, ten minutes from our home, as he was returning from two years at Oxford as a Rhodes scholar. Accustomed to the reverse flow of British traffic, he stepped in front of a truck. Now I knew a wrenching grief that fastened itself to me like a leech and wouldn't let go. In my twenty years as a parish pastor I had tried to help others with the pain of such festering grief. Now it was my turn to suffer.

Day after day, whenever I wasn't pressed with duties, I'd think of Paul. Never during his two years in England was I so preoccupied with him. Then, though separated by the Atlantic, I took him for granted. Now, separated by death, he became an obsession.

I had my faith. I believed that he still lived, now beyond another ocean. I believed that he was no longer oppressed by pain or meaninglessness or the prospect of death. In a sense, I knew he had "made it" in the fulfillment we all desired. Why then the pain?

A horde of questions attacked me. Like Jacob, who had loved Benjamin more than the others, had I loved Paul more than my other four sons and daughter? Were there things between Paul and me we should have cleared up, had we known the end was so near? What had I failed to do for him? Why should God let a promising young man die?

I felt grief and anger and remorse and guilt and loneliness. I cried to God. The Lord came with comfort, but it took time.

I had the most trouble with my anger. I resented the words of Job, "The Lord gave, and the Lord has taken away; may the name of the Lord be praised." I knew the Lord had given Paul to us, but I couldn't believe the Lord had arranged an accident to take him from us. I found myself angry, not at God, nor at the truck driver into whose path Paul had impulsively stepped. I was angry at the fallen order—in Omar Khayyam's words, "this sorry scheme of things entire," where sin and tragedy and accidents and illness and pain and death can thwart the greater plans of God for his children. I found comfort in thinking that God was indignant with this too, and that in a mixture of love and indignation he had sent his only Son to earth to put in motion a plan that would eventually set things right. I rediscovered a God who suffers with us.

I also learned the loneliness of grief. We are a tightly knit family, and we have a host of warm friends. We shared our grief. But grief leaves you on an island, quite alone. Even his mother and I could not really reach into the recesses of each other's grief. George Macdonald's words from *Diary of an Old Soul* I found to be true:

We all are lonely, Maker—each a soul
Shut in by itself, a sundered atom of thee.
No two yet loved themselves into a whole;
Even when we weep together we are two.

Guilt was not a serious problem. I could think of nothing serious that had come between us. Even if there were, I quickly reminded myself of the sweeping forgiveness of God that swallows up all our sins and removes them "as far as the east is from the west." Paul, now in heaven, and I, still on earth, could chuckle over anything that had marred our relationship, whatever that may have been.

Still, I felt it was virtually my duty to grieve. If I didn't grieve, had I loved him after all?

The magnificent picture in Hebrews came most to my rescue. In chapters 11–12 the writer parades the people who have died in their faith and who now, as victors, are in the celestial bleachers cheering us on.

> Therefore, since we are surrounded by such a great cloud of witnesses, let us throw off everything that hinders and the sin that so easily entangles, and let us run with perseverance the race marked out for us.

I pictured Paul in those bleachers, urging me to drop grief and return with zest to the common life and the joy of those around me.

It isn't as if grief ever quite lets go. But now, except for some swift, unexpected moments, when the loss surges in upon me again, the wrenching pain is gone. Some of life's mirth and merriment may be gone too. But sorrow becomes more like a minor chord in a symphony which, with the jubilant majors, combines to make a rich melody.

We do not belabor Paul's memory, nor avoid it. I occasionally wear his sweaters. We keep his pictures on display. Even his oar is resting against our bookcase, the oar he used in the Henley Regatta in the summer of 1960. It is at Christmas time that we miss him most. There are no presents for him or from him, nor his Christmas letter. We speak of what he might now have been doing. Sometimes I ponder what pain he may have been spared.

The passing of time helps, but it cannot fill the empty place. Fell a great tree, and a hole yawns against the skyline. No one ever takes another's place. All of us have a space in existence all our own. Our loss of Paul is indeed well flanked (twelve grandchildren have come since his death). Our other sons do not have their mother's brown eyes and black hair, but they and his sister all reincarnate some of Paul's exuberance and warmth.

When King David's little son was sick, the king fasted and prostrated himself before the Lord, and would not be comforted. The seventh day the child died. The servants hesitated to tell David that the child was dead, fearing that he would do himself harm. To their surprise, when he heard it, David washed himself, dressed, anointed himself, and sat down to eat. He told his servants, "While the child was still alive, I fasted and wept; for I said, 'Who knows? The Lord may be gracious to me and let the child live.' But now that he is dead; why should I fast? Can I bring him back again? I will go to him, but he will not return to me."

Paul sleeps in a little windswept graveyard on the prairies of South Dakota, next to his grandfather and grandmother. But he lives on in the fabric of the many lives he cherished and, I believe, ennobled. And with more than wistful longing, I believe that he lives and works in another part of the far-flung empire over which the Creator rules. I will go to him there. It is in the dimensions of that empire that grief comes tremulously to rest.

> *"You will grieve, but your grief will turn to joy."*
> *John 16:20*

7

When Death Is at the Door

"I'll never be afraid of death again," he said, and then added, "but you'll never know how wonderful it is just to be alive." We hadn't seen each other since he had recovered from the heart attack that the doctors had predicted would be fatal. I saw in him new serenity and new joy.

He had always been a man of faith, but, like most of us, he had not yet called on his faith in the face of imminent death. Now he knew what faith could do. He had passed the test, and his fear was gone.

I've been a bit puzzled, and not a little amused, at our preoccupation with "death and dying." Schools have courses of study on the subject, hospitals have workshops, congregations have series of talks. Usually a doctor, a lawyer, a funeral director, and a pastor are called in for their views—

as if, once you have put it together from these several perspectives, you're ready to go.

I'm not cynical about these studies. The doctor can detail the scientific story of death, the lawyer can tell you how to put your financial house in order, the funeral director can prepare you for some practical chores that will face your family. All this may help get you ready for the exit, and even give you some degree of comfort.

But death is the one experience in life that is different from all others. There's no rehearsal before the play is on. And, no matter how well you put your house in order by arranging your finances and even being reconciled to those you've wronged, it's what lies after death that cries for an answer. As Shakespeare's Hamlet says:

> The undiscovered country, from whose bourn
> No traveler returns, puzzles the will,
> And makes us rather bear those ills we have
> Than fly to others that we know not of.

Of course there's much comfort in thinking that you have done everything to make it easier for your family when you're gone. I pay $50 a year for an insurance policy that will yield my family $150,000 if I die in an airplane accident, and I must admit that when the flight is rough, I sit back and am comforted, knowing that if I die, my family will have more security than from my modest savings. And certainly, if you've been at odds with someone, there's comfort in becoming reconciled and having that dangling end tied up again.

But you expect to meet God on the other side. To come to terms with him is infinitely more important than to wrap up everything on this side.

A dying friend said, "Al, I'm not afraid to die, but I'm afraid to meet God, and you'll have to help me." He was a jurist, and it seemed absurd to him that God could forgive him and accept him in mercy. He said, "That's neither fair nor decent. We wouldn't handle wrongs in the lowest court of the land in such a shabby way." He felt that some sort of purgatory, either on this side or on the other side, would be necessary before God could accept him.

When at last the Lord overwhelmed him with the sheer mercy of grace in Christ Jesus, it was a dawn of a new day for him. But his legal intuition was right. It isn't just or even decent, for God to brush aside our wretched records and accept us in mercy. It is an act of pure love.

You'll never be able to gather up all the loose ends of your life and put them in order before you die. Get set as you will, something from the past will always haunt you. If there were no place to put the tangled snarls of your life, you'd be in trouble. But there is a place. God has provided it for you. It is at the foot of the cross, where Jesus Christ died for your sins, removing them "as far as the east is from the west."

Every one of us has a deep need for a place to rest, for someone to receive us "just as I am, without one plea, but that thy blood was shed for me, and that thou bidst me come to thee. . . ." The need is never greater than when we face the hour of death.

Instinctively we know that it will be absurd for us to stand before the high court of God and ask for justice: "Give me what I have coming, no more and no less." Before that bench each of us will have but one cry, "God, be merciful to me, a sinner."

Most of you, from the time you were children, have heard the story of God's mercy in Christ. But you may never have really understood the radical character of the story. You have felt that somehow, some way, you will have to prove yourself with God before God will take you in.

Now comes the hour of death. You know you haven't succeeded. There's too much unfinished business, too many dangling threads, too many neglects, too many hurts. Given a hundred years more, you still could not prove yourself before God.

You don't need to. God becomes not a judge, but a good and loving parent with a home waiting for you. All death can do is to open the door.

I like these lines from George Macdonald's *Diary of an Old Soul.*

> Yestereve, Death came, and knocked at my thin door.
> I from my window looked: the thing I saw,
> The shape uncouth, I had not seen before.
> I was disturbed—with fear, in sooth, not awe. . . .
> I was like Peter when he began to sink.
> To thee a new prayer therefore I have got—
> That, when Death comes in earnest to my door,
> Thou wouldst thyself go, when the latch doth click,
> And lead him to my room, up to my cot;
> Then hold thy child's hand, hold and leave him not,
> Till Death has done with him for evermore.

For the wages of sin is death, but the gift of God is eternal life in Christ Jesus our Lord.

    Romans 6:21

For Further Reading

I'm Thinking of You: Spiritual Letters of Hope and Healing
Herbert Brokering

All Will Be Well: A Gathering of Healing Prayers
edited by Lyn Klug

To Comfort and To Honor: A Guide to Personalizing Rituals for the Passing of a Loved One
Jeanne Daly McIntee

Good Grief
Granger E. Westberg
(Also available in large print)

When a Loved One Dies: Meditations for the Journey through Grief
Philip W. Williams

Winter Grief, Summer Grace: Returning to Life after a Loved One Dies
James E. Miller

The Color of the Night: Reflections on Suffering and the Book of Job
Gerhard E. Frost

Grieving the Death of a Friend
Harold Ivan Smith